JOURNEY TO
AMERICA

**Celebrating Inspiring Immigrants Who Became
Brilliant Scientists, Game-Changing Activists
& Amazing Entertainers**

Written and Illustrated by Maliha Abidi

becker&mayer! kids

Brimming with creative inspiration, how-to projects, and useful information to enrich your everyday life, quarto.com is a favorite destination for those pursuing their interests and passions.

© 2022 Quarto Publishing Group USA Inc.

This edition published in 2022 by becker&mayer! kids, an imprint of The Quarto Group, 11120 NE 33rd Place, Suite 201, Bellevue, WA 98004 USA.
(T)+1 425-827-7120 (F) +1 425-828-9659
www.Quarto.com

becker&mayer! kids titles are also available at discount for retail, wholesale, promotional, and bulk purchase. For details, contact the Special Sales Manager by email at specialsales@quarto.com or by mail at The Quarto Group, Attn: Special Sales Manager, 100 Cummings Center Suite 265D, Beverly, MA 01915 USA.

22 23 24 25 26   5 4 3 2 1

ISBN: 978-0-7603-7122-0

Library of Congress Control Number: 2021950392

Image Credits: p6-7: Science background © KamimiArt/Shutterstock; p11: Illustrated map © Leyasw/Shutterstock; p15: Hand drawn steamboat © Bonitas/Shutterstock; p23: Travel elements © Daria Pneva/Shutterstock; p24-5: Hand drawn Cinema set © Natasha Pankina/Shutterstock; p29: Set of Cinema food © Nina Novikova/Shutterstock; p37: Sketch books set © borsvelka/Shutterstock; p40: Cinema elements © Macrovector/Shutterstock; p45: Airplane isolated © natnatnat/Shutterstock; p48-9: Sports equipment © Ekaterina Mikheeva/Shutterstock; p50-1: Politics drawings © primiaou/Shutterstock; p59: Soldier hat © Natalia Hubbert/Shutterstock; p62: Treasury seal © Morphart Creation/Shutterstock; p64-5: Business drawings © primiaou/Shutterstock; p68: Office equipment © Ermakova Marina/Shutterstock; p72: Beverages © Aquarellka/Natalia Hubbert/PONOMARCHUK OLGA/Shutterstock; p74-5: USA drawn set © primiaou/Shutterstock; p79: Movie set © Aquarellka/Shutterstock; p87: Face Mask © nadiia_oborska/Shutterstock; p94: Ballot box © Yevgen Kravchenko/Shutterstock; p95: Question mark © MicroOne/Shutterstock;

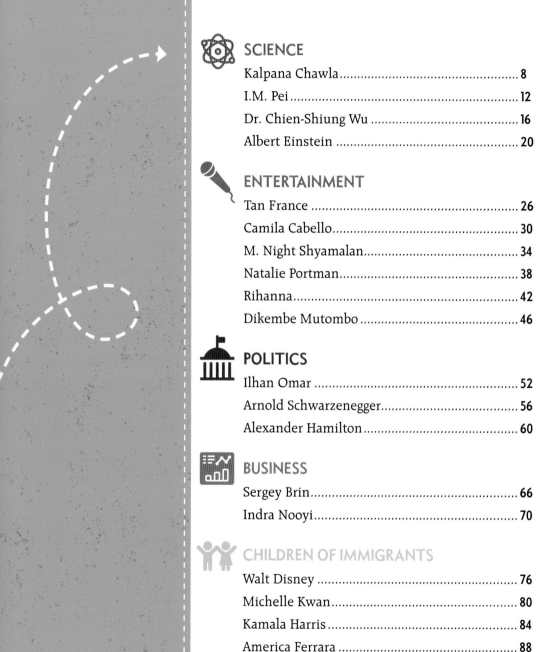

SCIENCE

ENTERTAINMENT

POLITICS

BUSINESS

CHILDREN OF IMMIGRANTS

WELCOME

Hello! My name is Maliha and this book, *Journey to America*, is a special project for me. This book is special not just because I am an immigrant who came to this country at age fourteen, but also because it allowed me to further appreciate the contributions of immigrants that made the United States of America what it is today.

As a Pakistani-American immigrant, I initially struggled with my identity. I asked, "Am I still Pakistani or am I American, now that I live here?" There was some guilt of letting go of an old life. I constantly felt homesick, and it was not an easy adjustment—especially given the cultural difference between the two countries. Something that helped me was the path paved by immigrants before me who set foundations in the U.S. and made sure future generations like myself can find themselves in this country. It is because of them that I can value both parts of my identity—the Pakistani side and the American side—and build something new.

While talking about the U.S., phrases such as "the melting pot" and "land of opportunities" are often used. The U.S. is a melting pot because people from around the world travel to this country and call it their home, and it has provided millions with opportunities. But it is also essential to remember the amazing innovators, artists, scientists, thinkers, and writers who brought their brilliant ideas to this land.

Millions of immigrants continue to contribute to the U.S. economy, culture, cuisine, and much more. They were brave enough to leave an entire life behind in their home country and start a journey in search of a better life for themselves and for their families. In that quest, the United States of America gained many great minds and hardworking citizens.

Journey to America consists of twenty stories of incredible people who positively contributed to the U.S., from Sergey Brin (the genius behind Google) to Rihanna (the talented musician, businesswoman, fashion icon, and philanthropist). This is a book, but it is also a small movement to remind people, through these stories, of the overall impact immigrants have had on the U.S. over the course of many decades and generations.

—Maliha Abidi

KALPANA CHAWLA

AEROSPACE ENGINEER AND ASTRONAUT

March 17, 1962 – February 1, 2003

Country of Origin: India

Kalpana's name means "imagination" in Sanskrit. She picked it for herself, and it was a fitting one indeed. Since she was a little girl, she imagined herself reaching for the stars.

Kalpana grew up in the town of Karnal, India. She often looked at the skies. During the day, she watched the planes passing over her home. During the night, she saw the stars, which fascinated her with their far-off shine.

As a child, Kalpana would make paper planes and pretend to be the pilot. Near her childhood home was a flight club. Kalpana asked her father all sorts of questions about the planes. One day her father arranged for her and her brother to get a ride on a plane. During the ride, Kalpana soared through the skies, and after she landed, she knew she wanted to fly high. She wanted to study engineering so she could achieve her ultimate goal of becoming an astronaut.

Kalpana decided to enroll in aeronautical engineering and became the first female student in the aeronautical engineering program at Punjab Engineering College. She graduated in 1982.

Kalpana moved to the U.S. to gain further knowledge in the field of aerospace engineering. She finished her Master of Science degree in 1984, followed by a PhD in aerospace engineering four years later. In 1988, she started working for NASA at the Ames Research Center. Kalpana loved her job and knew that she wanted to stay in the United States. In 1991, she became a U.S. citizen.

In a few short years, she was selected to be an astronaut. Kalpana went through tough training to prepare for her space travel, but she became the first Indian-born woman in space. She was a part of the STS-87 shuttle crew that conducted many space experiments, including multiple spacewalks. In 1997, she orbited the Earth 252 times before successfully returning home.

Kalpana was picked for another mission a few years later as part of a crew of seven astronauts. They traveled to space in the shuttle *Columbia* to conduct more experiments, but disaster struck when the shuttle began its descent toward the Earth. A piece of the aircraft broke off and damaged the heat shield, causing the spacecraft to break apart. None of the astronauts survived the disaster.

Kalpana left a great legacy. When she was growing up, there were no female astronauts in India. Now, because of the legacy she has left behind, millions of young children know they, too, can reach for the stars.

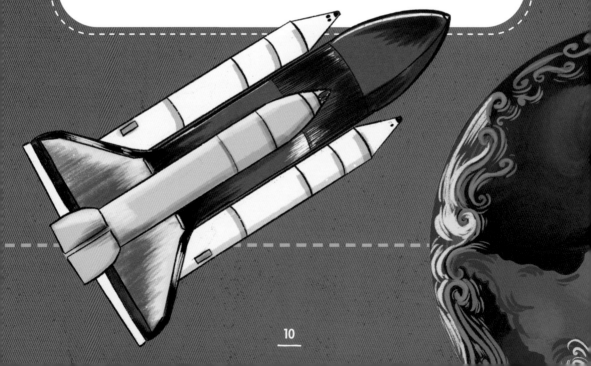

FROM HERE TO THERE, HUMANS WENT EVERYWHERE

Long before there were country borders, many human groups often moved from place to place. Geneticists, scientists who study what traits people inherit from their ancestors, have discovered that the first wave of American immigrants may have been a group of Ice Age wanderers who came across a small strip of land from Siberia about 20,000 years ago.

Early humans were constantly migrating. Sometimes they needed food, or maybe they wanted a different climate. Once civilizations became more stable, people migrated to explore or conquer new lands, or to escape war, enslavement, or persecution. People still migrate for some of these reasons today.

I.M. PEI

ARCHITECT

April 26, 1917 – May 16, 2019

Country of Origin: China

Ieoh Ming Pei, better known as I.M. Pei, was born in Guangzhou. A childhood spent in the big cities of Hong Kong and Shanghai inspired him to study architecture. His father wanted him to go to England, but he instead looked toward the United States of America.

Ieoh Ming boarded the SS President Coolidge ship with a student visa in his pocket and began his journey at eighteen. He didn't know how to speak English when he arrived, but his new friends welcomed him and taught him the language.

Ieoh Ming enrolled at the University of Pennsylvania to study architecture. As the course progressed, he realized it wasn't focused much on modern architecture, which Ieoh Ming was really interested in. He transferred to the Massachusetts Institute of Technology to continue his degree.

After graduating in 1940, Ieoh Ming thought about returning to China, but his father discouraged him. The political climate was changing quickly, and threats of war were on the rise. Ieoh Ming decided to study further and enrolled at Harvard Graduate School of Design to get his master's degree.

In the following years, Ieoh Ming became a superstar of the architecture world. He set up his firm, I.M. Pei & Associates, where he created many iconic buildings including:

The John F. Kennedy Presidential Library and Museum in Boston

The Rock and Roll Hall of Fame in Cleveland

The Bank of China Tower in Hong Kong

The Suzhou Museum in Suzhou

The Museum of Islamic Art in Doha

One of his best-known projects was the modernization of the Grand Louvre Museum in Paris. Impressed by Ieoh Ming's other buildings, President Mitterrand of France personally asked him to work on the Louvre Museum. Ieoh Ming didn't tell his firm about the project for several months because he wasn't sure if he would accept the commission. It was a big responsibility to work on such a historic site.

Ieoh Ming received a lot of criticism once the project was publicly announced. People objected to changing one of the most historically significant art museums in the world. But Ieoh Ming wasn't trying to change anything. His work would bridge historic and modern times. Eventually, the stunning glass pyramid at the Louvre was accepted by all.

Though Ieoh Ming was working on projects all over the globe, America was his home. In 1954, he became a citizen of the United States of America. Even though he was proud of his adopted home, he equally loved his original home, China. To strengthen the relationship between the two nations and to bring together a community of Chinese Americans, Ieoh Ming and his friend Dr. Henry Kissinger founded the Committee of 100, a group of influential Chinese Americans in business, government, academia, arts, and sciences.

From the Pritzker Architecture Prize of 1983 to the Presidential Medal of Freedom in 1992, I.M. Pei was a recipient of countless accolades and honors. A master of finding beauty in simplicity, he was a visionary and a pioneer of modern architecture.

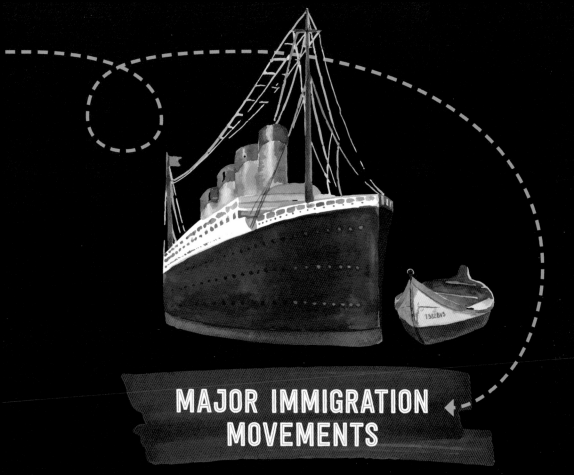

MAJOR IMMIGRATION MOVEMENTS

THE GREAT ATLANTIC MIGRATION: Though the United States was first settled by Europeans in the 1600s, it wasn't until the mid-1800s when mass populations crossed the Atlantic Ocean to settle in the new country. Between 1880 and 1910, seventeen million Europeans entered the United States.

THE RESETTLEMENT OF EUROPE: During and immediately after World War II, sixty million Europeans left their homes. Around 200,000 people (most of them fleeing Nazi Germany) came to the United States during the war.

DR. CHIEN-SHIUNG WU

PHYSICIST

May 31, 1912 – February 16, 1997

Country of Origin: China

Chien-Shiung Wu was born in the Jiangsu province in eastern China. Her parents believed in education for both boys and girls even though at the time, girls attending school was uncommon. When Chien-Shiung struggled to find a school to attend, her father started a school where she could prepare for university.

In 1936, Chien-Shiung sailed across the world to the United States of America to continue her studies in physics. She arrived in San Francisco and began her PhD at the University of California, Berkeley.

A few years after Chien-Shiung completed her degree, the world changed in the shadow of World War II. Alongside many brilliant minds from across the country, Dr. Wu was recruited to work on the top-secret Manhattan Project at Columbia University where she helped develop a method for separating uranium metal into U-235 and U-238 isotopes. For the remainder of her career, she stayed at Columbia University.

Dr. Wu made many great contributions to the field of physics, but some went uncredited. One of the most significant was in 1956. Two of her male colleagues approached her with their theory about disproving a quantum physics law that had been accepted for over thirty years. When her experiments disproved the law, her colleagues were recognized for the Nobel Prize in Physics. She was not.

After she was ignored, Dr. Wu said, "I wonder whether the tiny atoms and nuclei, or the mathematical symbols, or the DNA molecules have any preference for either masculine or feminine treatment." She often spoke up against the gender-based discrimination in the field of science. Though she wasn't recognized with the Nobel Prize, Dr. Wu didn't allow herself to be forgotten. She remains one of the most groundbreaking scientists whose work is still referenced and built on today.

AMERICA'S WELCOME WAGON

Ellis Island was an immigration station in the New York Harbor, very close to the Statue of Liberty. It welcomed almost twelve million immigrants to the United States between 1892 and 1954. Some immigrants nicknamed it the "Island of Hope," because it symbolized a new beginning and hope for a better life in America.

One of the most notable parts of immigrating through Ellis Island was a medical inspection. Each immigrant was tested for illness and interviewed to see if they would be able to support themselves financially. Those who passed both parts were welcomed to the country.

ALBERT EINSTEIN

THEORETICAL PHYSICIST

March 14, 1879 – April 18, 1955

Country of Origin: Germany

Albert Einstein moved around for a significant portion of his life. He was born in Ulm, Germany, and only six weeks after his birth, his family moved to Munich. They moved all over Europe, from Germany to Italy to Switzerland.

Even though Einstein mastered calculus on his own by the time he was fifteen, his teachers considered him an academic failure. In college, he would skip classes to spend more time experimenting in the lab. That may have been part of the reason he struggled to find a job as a professor and instead worked in the Swiss patent office. Still, he used his free time to experiment and develop theories.

In 1905, Einstein published his first paper, which was about the photoelectric effect. Only two months later, he published another paper that focused on the existence of the atom. Later that same year, he published a third paper about special relativity and a fourth paper about the famous $E=mc2$ equation.

Einstein received the Nobel Prize in physics in 1921 and quickly became so popular that he traveled globally to speak to scientists.

However, Einstein was a Jewish man, so his fame drew the attention of the Nazi regime in Germany. They put a price on his head, burned his books, and threatened his life. With Germany no longer safe for him, he traveled to England and eventually sailed to the United States.

Einstein was warmly welcomed in 1933, and he accepted one of many job offers as a professor at Princeton University. He said he would never return to his homeland because, "As long as I have any choice, I will stay only in a country where political liberty, toleration, and equality of all citizens before the law are the rule."

In 1940, Einstein became an American citizen, and he advocated for all citizens. He called racism "America's worst disease" and joined the National Association for the Advancement of Colored People (NAACP). He also worked with Black leaders such as Paul Robeson and W. E. B. Du Bois and campaigned for the American Crusade Against Lynching.

In his personal life, Einstein was a great lover of music (particularly songs by Mozart) and started playing the violin when he was six. He said he would have been a musician if he were not a physicist.

Though Einstein's best-known contributions were scientific, he touched many people in America and around the world with his writings on politics and the arts as well.

COMING AND GOING

This book is all about famous immigrants to America. But do you know the difference between "immigrants" and "emigrants?" Immigration is the process of coming into a new country, while emigration is the process of leaving an old country. Both words are based on "migrate," which means to travel among countries.

Here are some other words related to immigration.

DIASPORA means a people moving, voluntarily or not, outside their traditional homelands and making a new community there. For example, Chinese workers left China from 1850-1950 and in many of their new homes, their communities became known as Chinatown.

NOMADS are people who don't have a permanent home. Some ethnic groups are traditionally nomadic, such as the Romani travelers of Europe and the Bedouin people of the Arabian Peninsula.

ENTERTAINMENT

TAN FRANCE

FASHION DESIGNER, TELEVISION
PERSONALITY, AUTHOR

April 20, 1983

Country of Origin: England

Tanveer Safdar was born to Pakistani immigrants in England. His family lived in South Yorkshire county, in a predominantly white town where he was one of the only students of color at his school. When he was seven, he started working at his grandfather's factory during the summer, where he saw the manufacturing of denim clothes. By the time he was thirteen, he knew how to make pieces of clothing.

While Tan was growing up, he noticed how people saw white skin as the ideal. When a new baby was born in his family, the first question his relatives asked was, "How fair is the child?" Tan once found his cousin's skin bleaching cream and used it to try to be more accepted. However, he came to regret that act, when he realized his skin color was nothing to be ashamed of.

In school, Tan enrolled in psychology courses to please his family. But when he thought about the time he spent at his grandfather's factory and his love of clothing, Tan enrolled in a fashion college. When he informed his family, they were disappointed. All his other siblings had pursued a path in academia. To get their blessing, Tan convinced his family that he would be successful because he would be working in a field he truly loved.

True to his word, Tan went on to be a success in the fashion industry. After graduation, he worked at several fashion companies such as Zara and Chanel before starting his own company in 2011, Kingdom and State. He sold the business when he was thirty-three and retired from business.

Tan took his first trip to the United States when he was a teenager. Over the years, his job in fashion sent him to the country for up to six months at a time. When he was cast as the fashion expert on *Queer Eye*, he knew he might have to move permanently.

At first, Tan refused the position on *Queer Eye* because he was not an entertainer, but he wanted to represent his communities, as an openly gay, Muslim, South Asian man. On the show, Tan spoke about how he interacts with people who have never met a South Asian person before. He uses his position to break down their stereotypes.

Tan moved to America in 2015 and became an American citizen in 2020. Through fashion, he not only gives people makeovers and confidence, but he also starts conversations that advocate for unity and equality between communities around the world.

LIGHTS...CAMERA...
COME ON IN!

Have you ever heard one of your favorite actors talking and been surprised to hear a British accent? Many Hollywood stars grow up outside of the United States, then come to southern California for their big breaks.

This immigration is possible because of something called the O-1B visa. It is a temporary work visa designed for "individuals with extraordinary ability or achievement," in fields such as television, movies, theater, or the arts. However, because the definition of extraordinary achievement in the arts is vague, entertainers can take advantage of this type of visa.

Over half of Hollywood's O-1B petitions come from Britain!

CAMILA CABELLO

SINGER AND SONGWRITER

March 3, 1997

Country of Origin: Cuba

Camila said goodbye to her father when she was only six. The family had left Cuba, and Camila's father could only join her and her mother as far as Mexico because he didn't have a visa at the time. They weren't sure if the family would ever reunite, but they knew that going to America would be how Camila would achieve her dreams.

As they approached the Mexico-United States border, Camila held her mother's hand. Her mother, Sinuhe, was an architect who always kept a smile on her face, no matter how intimidating the journey was. Together, they rode a bus for hours, then waited at the border for twenty-two more hours.

Camila and her mother arrived in Miami where, for a while, they stayed with a good friend. Sinuhe worked in a shoe store, despite having had an entire career in architecture, and Camila started school. She didn't know the language, she had left all her friends in Cuba, and she was extremely shy. It took eighteen months before her father joined them, and her parents eventually started a construction company.

It was obvious from early on that Camila loved music. Her parents gifted her a karaoke machine when she was young, and her community would often get together to sing and dance. But as much as she liked to sing, she hated when people noticed her doing it. Sometimes she even cried.

But on YouTube, Camila could perform without being able to see the people watching her. She uploaded videos of her singing in private and shared them with the world. As more and more people liked her videos, Camila became more confident. One day, she saw a video about the TV show *X Factor* and decided to audition.

The audition was hours away, but that wouldn't stop Sinuhe and Camila. They'd already traveled so far.

At the audition, Camila spoke up when she was put in the alternates group. She overcame her shyness and convinced the judges to let her audition. They liked her so much that she made it to the next round, and she eventually became a member of a girl group called Fifth Harmony. After releasing albums and touring with them, Camila decided to pursue her own path.

From crossing borders to releasing music, Camila challenged herself to take risks, which led to her successful music career.

THE IMMIGRANT FAMILY TREE

According to the United States Census Bureau, immigrants who were born in another country are called first-generation immigrants. Their children, born in the United States, are called second-generation immigrants.

While immigrants face unique challenges as they get used to, or assimilate into, American culture, their children may also have a different experience than their American peers. Second-generation immigrants may need to balance the culture of their family at home with the American culture they experience at school or other activities.

M. NIGHT SHYAMALAN

FILMMAKER

August 6, 1970

Country of Origin: India

Manoj Nelliyattu Shyamalan was only an infant when, along with his parents, he migrated from India to Philadelphia, Pennsylvania, United States. His physician parents believed their family would have more opportunities in this country and hoped he would follow in their footsteps and pursue a career in medicine.

Manoj received a Super-8 camera when he was young, and by the time he was seventeen he had already made more than forty home movies. Something about writing stories and working with a camera struck him from the time he was a boy. He felt it was his destiny.

Manoj enrolled at New York University's Tisch School of the Arts to chase his dream of being a filmmaker. While he was still a student there, he made his first film *Praying with Anger.*

During college, he also chose to change his name from Manoj Nelliyattu to M. Night. In the years following, he faced prejudice against his "hard to pronounce" last name, with some publications referring to him with purposeful nonsense misspellings.

M. Night didn't let that stop him, and in 1999 he released his first hit, *The Sixth Sense.* It was nominated for numerous awards, including several Academy Awards nominations, and was the second highest grossing film of 1999. Fans and peers alike expected great things from M. Night, and he was one of the most successful directors making movies.

Even though some of his movies were criticized and some did not make a lot of money in ticket sales, M. Night never stopped creating. He kept doing what he loved, at times putting his own money into his projects. Eventually, he made a comeback with incredible movies that performed enormously well at the box office and restored people's faith in his work.

As a director of color in Hollywood, M. Night has faced challenges and judgment that others with his track record have not. But with his spirit of creativity and dedication to his craft, he has made a name for himself in Hollywood.

LIFE IN LITERATURE

In books, we can experience the lives of intergalactic astronauts or super-powered magicians. But we can also gain a better understanding of our neighbors. Immigrant authors reflect the ethnic diversity of America.

Through plays, poetry, novels, short stories, and nonfiction, hundreds of authors have expressed the reality of their immigration experience. One such author is Sandra Cisneros, a second-generation immigrant with a Mexican-born father, who credits her hybrid culture as the inspiration for her award-winning stories, such as *The House on Mango Street*.

NATALIE PORTMAN

ACTRESS

June 9, 1981

Country of Origin: Israel

Natalie Portman was born as Neta-Lee Hershlag in Jerusalem in 1981. On her mother's side, her family immigrated from Austria and Russia, and on her father's side, her ancestors moved to Israel from Poland and Romania. Her mother grew up in the United States before moving to Israel. In a family so used to moving, it was no surprise that they relocated to Maryland for her father's career when Natalie was three.

By 1991, the family was living in New York, where Natalie was approached by a talent scout. Natalie, who had always loved putting on shows at home, convinced her family to let her pursue acting. She scored her first professional performance in a play in 1993 and adopted the stage name of Natalie Portman to protect her privacy.

Natalie played various child roles in movies. Soon she landed the biggest role of her young career in *Star Wars Episode I: The Phantom Menace*, playing Queen Amidala. Despite how exciting the opportunity was, Natalie missed the premiere to stay home and study for a high school exam.

Her career was taking off as an actor, but she prioritized her education. Natalie graduated with honors from high school and attended Harvard University where she studied psychology. She starred in a huge variety of films, from blockbusters like *Thor* to Academy Award winners like *Black Swan*. Natalie has even directed films.

Off-camera, she cares about social justice and uses her celebrity to advocate for her causes. She spoke up about the gender pay gap in Hollywood and works with and contributes to organizations that help resolve human rights issues.

Natalie continues to lead by example, even turning down an award given by the Israeli government when she didn't agree with their policies. As a star on the screen and as an activist, Natalie has made the most of her life in America.

I PLEDGE ALLEGIANCE TO THE . . . FLAGS?

Even though most people consider themselves citizens of one country, it is possible to be citizens of more than one. This is called dual citizenship (two countries) or multiple citizenship (three or more countries). People with no citizenship are called stateless persons.

Some countries do not allow more than one citizenship and require their citizens to renounce, or give up, their other nationalities. Others may allow more than one citizenship with limited rights, such as not being able to serve in the armed forces.

Oscar-winning actress Charlize Theron has dual citizenship in both South Africa and the United States. She has been an activist in both countries and was even named a United Nations Messenger of Peace.

RIHANNA

SINGER AND BUSINESSWOMAN
February 20, 1988
Country of Origin: Barbados

Rihanna was born Robyn Rihanna Fenty, and she grew up in Saint Michael, Barbados with her parents and siblings. Her home life was so stressful that she used to get terrible headaches. The headaches didn't improve until her parents divorced when she was a teenager.

One of the most important things to Rihanna was the strength of the women in her family. She was especially close to her grandmother, whom she called Gran Gran Dolly. She also loved music, and she sang with two of her friends.

When she was sixteen, she was discovered in Barbados by an American music producer. For a while, she tried to attend school and record demos and write songs, but when it became clear that she was going to be successful, she decided to move to the United States.

Rihanna moved to the United States without her family and lived with her music producer and his wife. But as time went by, she missed her home. The title of her debut album, *Music of the Sun*, was inspired by the music of her sunny homeland, the Caribbean. Her first single, "Pon De Replay," also reflected her upbringing. Rihanna said that in Barbados, "Pon is 'on,' De means 'the,' so it's just basically telling the DJ to put my song on the replay."

The song definitely lived up to its name, and Rihanna shot up the music charts, scoring nine Grammy Awards and fourteen number one hits since 2006.

Outside of music, Rihanna has made strides in acting, business, and activism. Her first business venture was a fragrance in 2011, but she really made waves when she launched Fenty Beauty in 2017. The brand soon expanded with a line of undergarments. Rihanna created Fenty Beauty to challenge beauty standards and emphasize diversity, and she upheld that in everything from her fashion shows to her foundation colors.

Rihanna owns houses in multiple countries, including one in New York, but she considers herself a nomad. She loves the word immigrant, calling it a "prideful" word and saying that being an immigrant has made the world her oyster. That seems to be true because she has certainly gathered a legacy of pearls.

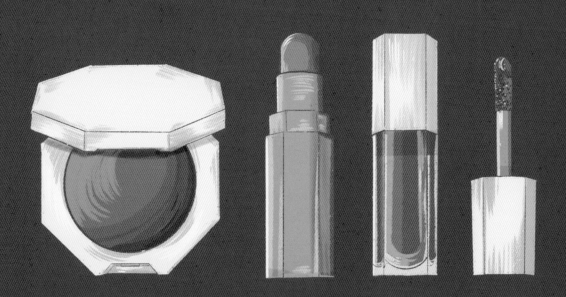

UNDOCUMENTED

One of the biggest topics in U.S. politics is immigration—specifically, illegal immigration. Undocumented immigrants do not have the paperwork that gives them the legal right to live in the country.

Some undocumented immigrants arrive secretly in the country, while others arrive legally to visit before deciding to stay past their deadline. Often, they do this because the process to become a legal citizen is very difficult, and their life in the new country is worth the risk of being deported or removed.

Many people, including musician Carlos Santana, oppose the strict action taken against undocumented immigrants, which can include sudden deportation that separates parents from children. Santana believes the immigration system needs to be reformed so that people seeking better lives are not punished unduly.

DIKEMBE MUTOMBO

BASKETBALL PLAYER

June 25, 1966

Country of Origin: Democratic Republic of the Congo

Dikembe was born in the city of Kinshasa, in the Democratic Republic of the Congo. Growing up, he was always taller than the kids his age, and people even bullied him for his height. He stopped going to the market because people would point and stare, making him feel that he didn't belong.

Some people said he looked like an American basketball player, but he didn't like playing basketball. He thought it was boring and preferred soccer. The first time he tried it, he smacked his head and had to get stitches on his chin. He practiced and got better, while also studying hard. Sometimes, when there was no electricity at his house, he would go to the nearby shops where there was light to do his homework.

At age twenty-one, he secured a college scholarship through the U.S. Agency for International Development and enrolled at Georgetown University.

During his second year at the university, the basketball coach recruited him. Even though he spoke almost no English, he was a valuable player known for blocking shots, and after graduating, Dikembe was drafted to the NBA's Denver Nuggets in 1991.

He had a legendary career as a defensive basketball player. His signature move was to wag his finger after blocking shots, making him a fan favorite as well. Throughout his eighteen-year NBA career, he won eight NBA All-Star titles and four NBA Defensive Player of the Year Awards.

Dikembe used his influence and resources to build a hospital in Kinshasa. He named it the Biamba Marie Mutombo Hospital after his mother.

Dikembe exceled at everything. He was an educated man who graduated from a top institution with degrees in Linguistics and Diplomacy, a successful professional basketball player inducted in the NBA Hall of Fame in 2015, and a philanthropist who showcased the importance of giving back to the community. An all-star in life and on the basketball court.

ONE, TWO, THREE STRIKES, YOU'RE IN!

Baseball: America's Pastime. The sport is as American as apple pie, right? Well, despite it being almost exclusively played in the United States, around a quarter of Major League Baseball players are foreign-born. These players come from the Dominican Republic, Venezuela, Cuba, Mexico, and many other countries.

The teams help the players they want to sign, or add to the team, get a P-1 visa during their contracts. If the athlete wants to remain permanently, the teams can help them get permanent residence (see page 55) on a EB-1 or EB-2 visa for extraordinary or exceptional ability.

Bartolo Colón is one such Dominican-born baseball player who became a U.S. citizen in 2014 during his successful pitching career. As a mentor and a role model for many young baseball players, he has given as much to young U.S. athletes as he has to his old community of Altamira, Dominican Republic.

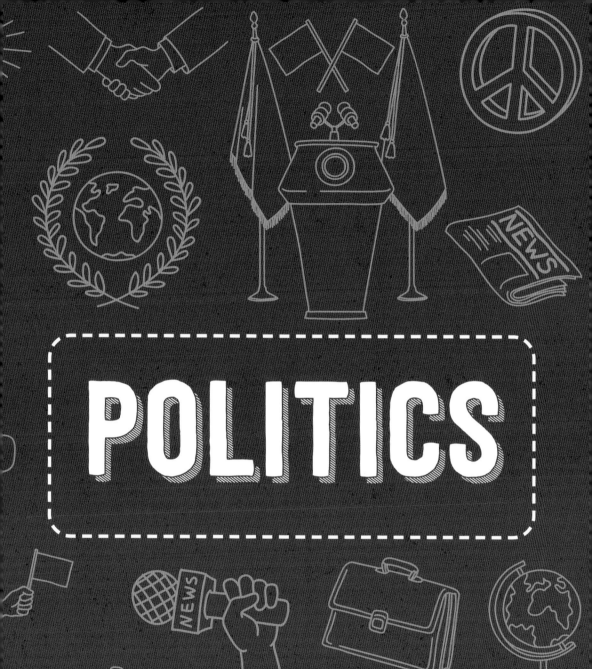

POLITICS

ILHAN OMAR

CONGRESSWOMAN

October 4, 1982

Country of Origin: Somalia

Ilhan was born in Mogadishu, the capital of Somalia. She lost her mother when she was only two, but her father was always there with her. Her childhood was full of family, as she was the youngest of seven children.

When Ilhan was eight, everything changed when war broke out. It was no longer safe for Ilhan and her family to stay in Somalia. The country she loved was changing in front of her eyes. She said goodbye to her home and fled with her family to a Kenyan refugee camp.

New problems awaited her family in the refugee camp. People didn't have enough food to eat, rarely had any clean drinking water, and often got sick. Her father spoke often about America. A glimmer of hope. A land where they would be safe and free.

While they wished for change, life in the refugee camp was not easy. Ilhan went hungry, and she lived amongst great poverty. But she and her family never lost hope, and four years later, they were cleared to board a plane to America.

In 1995, Ilhan lived in Virginia before moving to Minnesota. Her family settled in the Cedar-Riverside neighborhood of Minneapolis, an area that welcomed a large number of Somali immigrants fleeing the civil war.

When she first came to the U.S., Ilhan had a hard time making friends because she didn't speak English. But as she learned the language, she made friends and found great connections in the community. In 2000, she officially became a U.S. citizen.

With her brand new English skills, Ilhan attended public political events with her grandpa as his interpreter. During these events, Ilhan became interested in politics. In college, she studied political science and international studies at North Dakota State University. She was also a community educator at the University of Minnesota and regularly met with activists to discuss issues close to her heart, such as climate change, student debt, and health care. Ilhan wanted to help people who were sometimes overlooked.

In 2018, Ilhan became a congresswoman. She made history as the first Somali American, and one of the first two Muslim women, elected to serve in Congress.

As a refugee and an immigrant, Ilhan represents and inspires the people whose lives she is dedicated to improving.

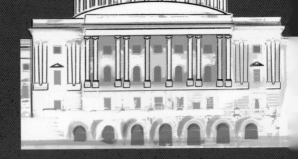

United States of America
Permanent Resident

Surname
Shah
Given Name
Faizah Shah
USCIS#   Category
Country of Birth
Pakistan
Date of Birth
11 Jan 2003   Sex
                                E
Card expires
06/08/2025
Resident since
08/08/2020

CHECK YOUR STATUS: TYPES OF IMMIGRANTS

1. **LAWFUL PERMANENT RESIDENT (LPR):** This describes someone legally allowed to live and work in the United States. It is said these people have a "green card," because these identification papers were colored green from 1946-1964. LPRs are not eligible for certain benefits, such as voting, but they can become citizens after five years and passing a citizenship test.

2. **TEMPORARY VISITOR:** Sometimes people come to the United States on a visa, which lets them live in the country for a period of time, such as for a college education. If the visitor remains in the country after the visa expires, they are no longer legally visiting.

3. **UNDOCUMENTED IMMIGRANT:** This is someone who has come to the country without the proper paperwork. This type of person is at risk of being deported, which means being sent back to the country they came from.

ARNOLD SCHWARZENEGGER

BODYBUILDER, MOVIE STAR, POLITICIAN

July 30, 1947

Country of Origin: Austria

Imagine if you had to do sit-ups before you could eat your breakfast. That was reality for Arnold Schwarzenegger, who was born to a strict father who focused on his children's physical fitness. Arnold's first sport was soccer, and when he was fifteen, he started lifting weights to get better on the field. In the gym, he was inspired by the bodybuilders and soon tried to shape his body like he saw them doing.

During his year of mandatory service in the Austrian army, he signed up for the Junior Mr. Europe contest, and when he didn't get permission to leave the army, he went anyway. He spent a week in jail for sneaking away, but it didn't matter. Arnold had won the competition, and a year later, he became the youngest winner of the Mr. Universe contest.

There were more opportunities for bodybuilders in the United States, so Arnold moved to California without speaking English. He won so many bodybuilding contests that people took notice. Arnold, who always wanted to try acting in movies, took advantage of his popularity and his distinct look to audition for roles. But casting agents said he was too big, his accent was too strong, and even his long name wasn't right for the silver screen.

Arnold knew that to be successful as an actor, he wouldn't have to change himself. Instead, he would become his very best self and prove that he was right for big roles. He won the biggest bodybuilding contest in the world, Mr. Olympia, seven times and even starred in a documentary about bodybuilding.

And finally, Hollywood noticed. His breakthrough role was in 1982's *Conan the Barbarian*, a role that showed off his size, his accent, and his long name. He became known for his ability to be an action hero with a sense of humor, which set him apart in movies.

But Arnold wasn't done yet. The bodybuilder and movie star loved the country he had moved to. He made his way into politics from a role on the California Governor's Council on Physical Fitness and Sports before eventually running for governor of California and being elected in 2003.

A star in three fields, Arnold is one of the most famous and successful immigrants the United States has ever seen.

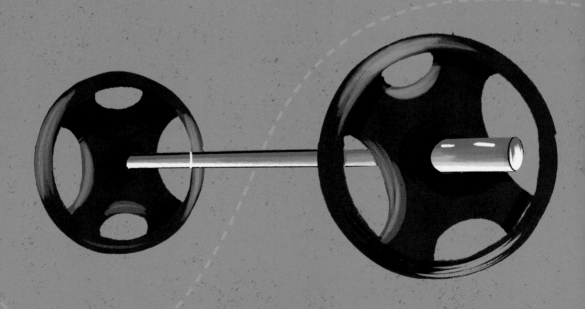

FIGHTING FOR YOUR (FUTURE) COUNTRY

Even though the military is often referred to as "those brave Americans," some enlisted members of the armed forces are non-citizens. More than 30,000 active duty members of the military are immigrants, and since 2002, the U.S. has expedited over 139,000 citizenships for military members.

On the other side of military immigration, many deployed soldiers living in other countries meet and marry locals. That was the case for Senator Tammy Duckworth, whose American marine father met her Thai Chinese mother while stationed in Thailand during the Vietnam War. The senator has American citizenship through her father, which allowed her to run for U.S. political office.

ALEXANDER HAMILTON

FOUNDING FATHER

January 11, 1755 or 1757-July 12, 1804

Country of Origin: Nevis

In the 1700s, many people immigrated to the Americas, but Alexander Hamilton's journey was unique. He was born on a small island in the British West Indies called Nevis. After this father left the family and his mother died when Alexander was young, he got his first job around age eleven as an accounting clerk, where he practiced reading, writing, and business.

He became so good at writing that he published poems and letters in a local newspaper. One letter, about a recent hurricane, impressed people so much that they paid for him to go to the American colonies and get an education.

When Hamilton arrived in New York, the American colonies were getting ready for war against the British. Always opinionated, he got involved, writing pamphlets to convince colonists to fight for their independence. His accomplishments in the army caught the eye of General George Washington, who invited Alexander to become a part of his staff.

Once the war ended, and the American colonies were officially independent, Alexander knew the work was just beginning. He didn't think the nation would succeed unless all the states worked together, so he returned to New York to try to help make a strong central government. To do that, he helped write essays to convince the American people that such a government was needed. Alexander wrote fifty-one of the eighty-five Federalist Papers.

Thanks in part to Alexander, the government was established, with George Washington as the first president. He named Alexander as Secretary of the Treasury, and Alexander was tasked with finding a way to pay off the country's debt after the war. He did this by proposing the first Bank of the United States.

A persuasive writer and passionate patriot, Alexander Hamilton was one of America's most influential Founding Fathers—and he worked hard to move up the ladder of power. Today he is honored with a place on our currency (he's on the $10 bill!), and remembered in *Hamilton*, an award-winning musical that celebrates diversity and the contributions of immigrants by casting multicultural actors in the majority of the roles.

AN ASYLUM TO THE PERSECUTED

America's Founding Fathers imagined the country as a safe place for refugees and immigrants. The Declaration of Independence signers even criticized the British king for blocking immigration.

President George Washington wrote, "I had always hoped that this land might become a safe and agreeable asylum to the virtuous and persecuted part of mankind, to whatever nation they might belong," promising refugees a home in America.

Through immigration, America has multiplied its population many times, leading to a "melting pot" of global cultures.

BUSINESS

SERGEY BRIN

COMPUTER SCIENTIST AND ENTREPRENEUR

August 21, 1973

Country of Origin: Russia

When Sergey's father was growing up in Russia, he dreamed of becoming an astrophysicist. But he wasn't allowed to study physics in graduate school because he was Jewish. When Sergey was six, in 1979, he and his mom, dad, and grandmother were able to get exit visas and leave the country so that his family could have more opportunities.

Sergey's first memory of the United States was looking at all the huge cars driving past on the highway. His family settled in Maryland, with his father becoming a math professor and his mother working as a researcher at NASA.

When Sergey first started school, he struggled to speak in English with his classmates. But he was good at math and computers—so good that when he grew up, he earned degrees in computer science and mathematics at the University of Maryland, then went to Stanford University for graduate school. In California, Sergey tried all type of sports like gymnastics, rollerblading, skating, swimming, skiing, and trapeze!

When he was at Stanford, Sergey met Larry Page and the two started working together on a project in Larry's dorm room (which soon expanded into Sergey's dorm room). It was a new type of search engine that would rank websites based on how many other pages linked to them. At first they called their search engine BackRub, but soon changed it to Google. "Google" was misspelled from "googol," which is the math term for the number one followed by one hundred zeros!

At Google, Sergey worked on projects like self-driving cars, smart glasses, and even smart contact lenses. He was also interested in using technology to solve problems like climate change and to find sources for renewable energy. Today, he is one of the richest people in the world.

In 2017, Sergey used his experience as an immigrant to speak up against a ban on immigrants from Muslim countries. "The U.S. had the courage to take me and my family in as refugees," he said. Without that opportunity, "I wouldn't be where I am today or have any kind of the life that I have today."

Sergey describes himself as "kind of a weirdo," but sometimes it takes a person with a different perspective to see what others may not see and to create innovative ideas.

WE MEAN BUSINESS

Some of the most successful American brand names were started by immigrants . Levi Strauss, a name now famous with jeans, was born in Germany in 1829 before moving to the United States at age eighteen. He worked at a dry goods business in Manhattan with his family before striking out to open a new branch of the business in California. There, he found that tent canvas worked well to make sturdy pants for the miners.

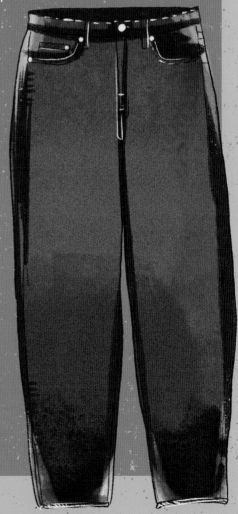

Many immigrants risk a lot to move to America, especially centuries ago when travel was more difficult. Maybe these difficulties influenced their decisions to take another chance on starting a business. Or maybe they came to America because it was a land of opportunity, and their dream was to start their own business. Why do you think so many immigrants started successful businesses?

INDRA NOOYI

BUSINESSWOMAN, CEO

October 28, 1955

Country of Origin: India

Growing up, Indra's mother would ask her and her sister to present a speech after dinner. They would pretend to be a different world leader, such as a president or a prime minister. Depending on their speech, their mother would decide who she would vote for. This nightly activity inspired Indra to become a strong leader.

Indra was born and raised in Madras, India (now called Chennai). Her family was not wealthy, but they had enough to support Indra's goals. Growing up, she sang, played the guitar, played cricket, climbed the trees, and was a bright student at school. She was expected to get good grades, receive at least a master's degree, and be married by the age of eighteen.

Indra was accepted into the prestigious Indian Institute of Management Calcutta, where she received her MBA. She was one of only a handful of female students accepted, something she became used to during her life.

After graduation, she wanted to study more in the United States. Her family had other plans for her. They wanted her to get married. It was unusual for a girl of her background to go abroad on her own, especially if she was unmarried. But Indra's persuasive speech convinced her parents to allow her to attend Yale School of Management.

When Indra arrived in New Haven, Connecticut in 1978, everything was foreign to her. Once again, she was in a place where only a few people were like her. The initial days of coming to a new country and settling in were tough, but she had big goals and focusing on them helped her get used to her new home.

When Indra first began working, she only had two suits to wear, a black one and a beige one. She was creative with the way she wore them, styling the two suits in four ways. She looked and dressed differently from her coworkers, but by now she was used to that.

In 1994, Indra joined PepsiCo. She focused on working hard and rose from vice president all the way to CEO in 2006. At that time, there were only a dozen female CEOs of Fortune 500 companies.

It was difficult at times to find a balance between running a company and being a mother, but Indra did it all with grace, even bringing her two daughters to the office with her. A girl from India became one of the most powerful businesswomen in the United States and remained CEO of PepsiCo for twelve years, proving that different can mean exceptional.

EATING AROUND THE WORLD

Did you know pizza comes from Italy? Or that ramen originated in China? Have you tried falafel from Egypt or pierogi from Poland? What about crepes from France or mochi from Japan?

Food is a universal language—and it's delicious, too! A common business for immigrants to start is a local restaurant. Many ethnic foods have been introduced to America by families bringing their recipes to the United States. Some studies say immigrants own almost 30% of restaurants and hotels across the country.

What's your favorite type of food? Where in the world did it come from?

CHILDREN OF IMMIGRANTS

WALT DISNEY

ENTREPRENEUR AND ANIMATOR

December 5, 1901 – December 15, 1966

In the 1800s, nearly seventeen million Europeans immigrated to the Americas. The Disneys were one such family. Walt Disney was born to an Irish Canadian father and a German American mother in Chicago, before his family moved him and his siblings to a small town in Missouri.

Walt loved the magic of small towns, but he also loved the arts. He saw his first circus parade and his first motion picture in Marceline, Missouri, which stuck with him for years. He even sold his first piece of artwork as a child in that town.

Growing up, Walt worked hard. He had a paper route as a child and even dropped out of school to try to enlist in World War I when he was only sixteen (though he wasn't accepted due to his age). Determined to help in the war effort, he lied about his age to join the Red Cross.

At eighteen, Walt got his first art job, and after producing commercial illustrations for advertising, he met Ub Iwerks, another artist. Together, they started an art company, and Walt decided that animation was the future. In 1923, Walt, his brother Roy, and Iwerks moved to Hollywood with a suitcase and a dream.

Mickey Mouse made his cartoon debut in 1928 with the animated short film *Steamboat Willie*. Walt became a pioneer in animation, creating early successes that matched sound with picture, but his biggest innovation was an animated feature film released in 1937 called *Snow White and the Seven Dwarfs*. No one believed it would stand up to live action movies, but it became one of the biggest successes in cinema at that time.

But Walt wasn't done taking risks. In 1955, he took all of his amazing storytelling and opened Disneyland, a theme park whose centerpiece was partially based on the small town where he grew up.

With twenty-two Oscars and a legacy that resounds around the world, Walt Disney believed in achieving the impossible—no matter where you come from.

INBETWEENERS

In addition to his own status as a child of immigrants, Walt Disney employed many immigrants in the early days of the studios. One talented worker was Chinese American Tyrus Wong, who started as an inbetweener, the job title for the person making the in-between drawings that link key shots in animated films together.

Wong's most recognizable contribution to the Disney catalog was in *Bambi*, where he brought his beautiful art style to the film, inspired by the lush Song dynasty landscape paintings.

Wong may have started his career in America as an inbetweener, in more ways than one, but he finished it as a Disney Legend whose work influences animators even today.

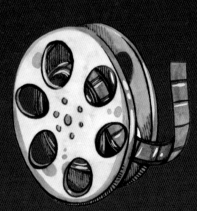

MICHELLE KWAN

FIGURE SKATER, OLYMPIAN

July 7, 1980

There have been two major waves of immigration from Asia to America. The first large wave of immigrants arrived in the mid-1800s and worked hard on railroads and in mines. The second wave started around 1965, after the United States and China changed immigration policies. Michelle Kwan's parents were part of the second wave, arriving in California from Hong Kong in the early 1970s.

As the third child, Michelle always wanted to keep up with her older brother and sister, both of whom enjoyed ice sports. She soon joined the ice rink herself, which was tough on her middle-class parents because the sport was expensive. But they made sure Michelle could chase her dreams, even if they had to sew her ice skating costumes at home.

When her mother was working multiple jobs, she would stay up all night to sew sequins onto Michelle's leotards. Sometimes, Michelle would see this, and she knew she had to train hard enough to make her parents' sacrifices worth it. She was good enough that her local skating foundation paid for her coaching. Michelle committed to ice skating fully, even becoming homeschooled in eighth grade to focus on her training. She surprised her coach by taking the test to become a senior-level skater when she was only twelve years old.

Michelle won her first world championship title in 1996, at age fifteen, but her real goal was the Olympics. In 1998, she won a silver medal and in 2002, a bronze medal. During her almost decade-long international career, Michelle earned five world championship titles, tying her for the most ever by an American.

Michelle was so stunning on the ice that top designer and fellow daughter of Chinese immigrants Vera Wang wanted to make her costumes. Vera called Michelle "an actress on the ice" and the pair became close friends, even after Michelle's skating career.

After Michelle retired from skating, she took advantage of her studies in Asian history and politics and became the first U.S. Public Diplomacy Envoy, a position that allowed her to travel and start conversations with youth around the world. Today, she works in politics, advocating for gender equality, sports diplomacy, and diversity in athletics.

FASTER, HIGHER, STRONGER – TOGETHER

"Faster, Higher, Stronger—Together," that's the Olympic motto. In 2015 the International Olympic Committee created the Refugee Olympic Team. In Rio in 2016, ten athletes displaced from countries such as Ethiopia, Syria, and South Sudan competed in various events.

One displaced athlete was swimmer Yusra Mardini, who fled Syria after her house was destroyed in the civil war. While being smuggled to Greece by boat, their dinghy began to sink. Yusra treaded water for over three hours to keep those who could not swim safe. Yusra is now settled in Germany.

KAMALA HARRIS

VICE PRESIDENT OF THE UNITED STATES OF AMERICA

October 20, 1964

In the years since Kamala was born, the United States of America has changed and progressed a lot. The year she was born, legal segregation ended, and soon after, the voting rights act of 1965 was passed, outlawing discriminatory voting practices. In her lifetime, she saw the first Black president of the United States, Barack Obama, be elected. She was part of the second-ever class of racially integrated public schools in Berkeley, California. Kamala's journey puts into perspective how many historic changes took place in a matter of decades. It's only fitting that Harris made history as the first female vice president of the United States in 2020.

The daughter of a cancer researcher from India, Shyamala Gopalan, and an economist from Jamaica, Donald Harris, Kamala was born in Oakland, California. Her mother chose a name with Indian origins that means "Lotus," and hoped that her daughter would bloom.

Growing up, Kamala often accompanied her parents to civil rights protests, which taught her to always stand up for justice and equality. Her parents divorced when Kamala was only seven, and she was raised by her mother. Shyamala made sure to teach Kamala about both parts of her heritage, and her goal was to raise a strong woman.

On a trip to India, Kamala learned more about how her grandparents were also social justice activists who stood up and fought for India's independence.

Kamala received a degree in political science and economics from Howard University, followed by a degree from the University of California, Hastings College of the Law. She was the first Black woman in California to be elected as district attorney and went on to become attorney general of California.

Trailblazer Kamala Harris made history when she was picked to be the running mate for Joseph Biden. She broke multiple glass ceilings all at once when she became the first female vice president, the first Black vice president, and the first Indian vice president of the United States of America.

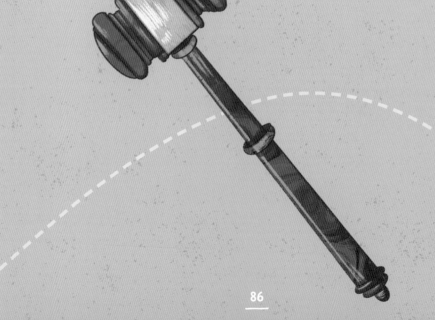

COVID-19 AND
THE AMERICAN DREAM

Coronavirus, a worldwide pandemic that began in 2019, had a worldwide response to help stop its spread. Three of the companies that were most successful in developing a vaccine were all founded by immigrants.

U.S. company Pfizer was founded by an immigrant from Germany, and has a Greek CEO. Moderna, also based in the U.S., was co-founded by immigrants from Canada and Lebanon.

International problems are solved by international solutions, and global cooperation is one of the many things helping to limit COVID-19.

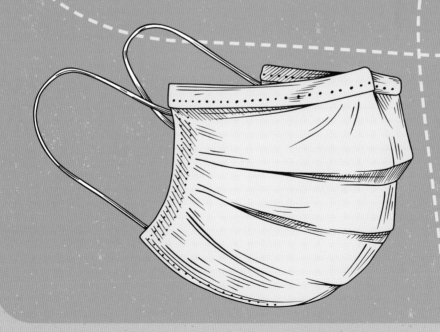

AMERICA FERRERA
ACTRESS AND ACTIVIST
April 18, 1984

"I am American. My name is America."

This is what America, an aspiring actress at the time, told the world when she faced rejection in show business because of her ethnicity.

Born and raised in Los Angeles, America lived with her siblings and their mother, who was an immigrant from Honduras. Growing up next door to Hollywood, America always had big dreams of becoming an actress. She went to her first audition when she was fifteen, where she realized she was one of very few Latina actors in television and movies. Casting agents and directors told her Latina main characters wouldn't be watched by the public, so studios wouldn't risk hiring Latina actors for big roles. She was stuck in stereotypical parts.

But America dreamed of a world where she, and girls like her, could see themselves in media. And finally, she scored a part in *Real Women Have Curves*, which was about a Latina girl who wanted to convince her family to support her in college. This was close to America's real life, because she was a college student on a scholarship to the University of Southern California. A professor told her that his Latina student had recommended that he watch *Real Women Have Curves* to help him understand the student's life. When she heard this, America knew that all her hard work for representation had been worth it.

America booked larger and larger roles, including a main character on the TV show *Ugly Betty*, for which she became the first Latina to win a lead actress Emmy.

America's dream of becoming an actress had come true, but her success also meant that millions of people finally saw themselves on screen in her roles in television and film.

GET INVOLVED!

As the laws surrounding immigration continue to change, many Americans (both natural-born citizens and immigrants) are making their voices heard. Many organizations have organized campaigns, marches, and debates across the country to make sure lawmakers hear what immigrants have to say.

There are even youth-led groups, such as United We Dream, which empower children and teens to understand the laws and needs of immigrant people. Visit them at www.unitedwedream.org

BARACK OBAMA
44TH PRESIDENT OF THE UNITED STATES
August 4, 1961

Barack was born in Hawaii to a Kenyan father and an American mother. His parents separated when he was an infant, and he only met his father once when he was ten. Raised by his mother and maternal grandparents, Barack's upbringing was a typical American childhood. In the 1960s when the political climate was changing radically in the U.S., his mother, Stanley Ann, made sure to educate and inform her son of social issues.

When Barack was young, his mother married an Indonesian man and Barack spent his early childhood years with them in Indonesia. He returned to the United States at the age of ten. His mother and grandparents weren't wealthy, but they made sure Barack got the best education. He studied at Punahou, a top prep school in Hawaii. In high school Barack asked himself questions related to race and class. His experiences of being raised by a single mother, living in Hawaii where not many people looked like him, and then moving to Asia where, again, not many people looked like him, and his observations about the disparity in class shaped his early years. He didn't share these thoughts with anyone because he didn't want to stand out even more than he already did. Books became his escape and he would often lose himself in the pages of stories, a habit his mother helped nurture.

Barack's years at Occidental College made him realize the importance of people coming together to influence and create change. He studied great minds from history and civil rights movements such as Lech Wałęsa, John Lewis, Bob Moses, and many others.

Barack transferred from Occidental College to Columbia University in New York. After he graduated from Columbia, the call to serve the people took him to Chicago, where he worked with communities devastated by homelessness, poverty, and joblessness. A few years later, he was admitted to Harvard Law School and became the first Black president of the *Harvard Law Review*.

After working as a law school professor and a state senator, Barack ran for president and in 2008 became the first African American president ever. He served for two terms, leading a country dealing with a financial crisis, and once again, rising as a leader as he had done so on many occasions before. He served for two terms from January 2009 to January 2017.

Barack is a best-selling author, Nobel Peace Prize winner, and even a two-time Grammy winner for his audiobooks.